RAINWATER HAIR

poems by

Steve Brammell

Finishing Line Press
Georgetown, Kentucky

RAINWATER HAIR

Copyright © 2023 by Steve Brammell
ISBN 979-8-88838-099-4 First Edition
All rights reserved under International and Pan-American Copyright Conventions. No part of this book may be reproduced in any manner whatsoever without written permission from the publisher, except in the case of brief quotations embodied in critical articles and reviews.

ACKNOWLEDGMENTS

Rainwater Hair, Corn Truck Overturns on Main Street, and Cuban Missile Crisis Anxiety appeared in *The Flying Island Journal*
Olive, Dishwasher, Orange, Crows, Boat Hull Moving Party In A Small Town, Canada Geese, Road, and Chimney Swifts At Night appeared in *The Write Launch*
Crow Haiku appeared in *Narrative Northeast*
Baptism in the Dead Sea appeared in *The Northwest Indiana Literary Journal*
The Old Man Speaks at Commencement appeared in *Cathexis Northwest Press*
Ancestors appeared in *The Ravensperch*
Leg Cramp At Night appeared in the *White Wall Review*
Ode to Sand, Old Sycamore, Swarm, Running the Trails at Eagle Creek, Migrating Sandhill Cranes, Children of Fire, The Creek, and Sunny Morning After the Big Blizzard appeared in *The Tiny Seed Literary Journal*
Bloodroot first appeared in *Birmingham Magazine*

Publisher: Leah Huete de Maines
Editor: Christen Kincaid
Cover Art: Steve Brammell
Author Photo: Steve Brammell
Cover Design: Elizabeth Maines McCleavy

Order online: www.finishinglinepress.com
also available on amazon.com

Author inquiries and mail orders:
Finishing Line Press
PO Box 1626
Georgetown, Kentucky 40324
USA

Table of Contents

Olive 1

Baptism In The Dead Sea 3

Migrating Sandhill Cranes 4

Cuban Missile Crisis Anxiety 5

Children Of Fire 6

Rainwater Hair 8

Chimney Swifts At Dusk 10

Corn Truck Overturns On Main Street 11

Sunny Morning After The Big Blizzard 12

Ode To Sand 13

Orange 16

Ancestors 17

Dishwasher 20

Canada Geese 21

The Creek 22

Road 24

Old Sycamore 25

Boat Hull Moving Party In A Small Town 26

Running The Trails At Eagle Creek 27

The Old Man Speaks At Commencement 29

Swarm 30

Four Haiku 31

Crows 32

Leg Cramp At Night 33

Bloodroot 34

OLIVE

> *It is among the oldest cultivated trees in the world, being grown before written language was invented.*
> —History of the Olive

Who was the first to try
an olive ripe from the tree,
the paltry flesh over stony seed
so bitter it must be poison?

Who learned the magic
to make it succulent?

Sun cured or covered in salt,
soaked in brine or lye,
the months waited
with an ancient's trust in miracles,

Washed, then crushed, the pits removed,
pulp placed in woven bags and baskets
and pressed for gold/green oil
hiding in plain sight,
the last drops coaxed from the dregs
with boiling water.

Full vats, amphorae lining walls,
riding in the holds of ships with many oars,
feeding flames of lamps and altars,
ointments rubbed by healers' hands,
anointing poets, warriors, kings,
and the Chosen with their haloes.

Sun and rock, the old ones say,
drought and silence and solitude—
this is what the olive needs to thrive,
to provide for those who tend her
in these promised lands.

Her trunk delights in twisting,
her branches keep low and tangled—
in spite she lives for centuries.

Devoted generations stay home
and lie in her shade,
feel their blood
pushing up from her roots,
vessels for her spirit
when they dance without care
after the harvest.

BAPTISM IN THE DEAD SEA

The stones on the bottom
were slippery,
the water like oil
against my legs—
this sea where you cannot drown.

A single tourist
floated upright
as if lounging in a chair.

I understood
there would be no preacher
with a hand under my back
and scripture to welcome
me up from the grave.

I dove in head first,
kept my eyes closed as warned,
stayed down with full lungs
but felt a buoyancy
try to expel me
as though some secret
farther down needed guarding.

I broke through the surface,
a split second of sight
to witness what I hoped
would be a sinless world,
then the salt on my face
got into those wandering eyes
and I knew the old God
still reigned in the lowest place on earth,
blinding me
for the curiosity
that brought me here,

my skin glittering
like Lot's wife
the rest of the day
as I tried to find
fresh water.

MIGRATING SANDHILL CRANES

Their calls pierce
shingles and wood,
even concrete held by steel,
to find me deep inside
my ordinary life.

I rush outside if I can,
those who know
my peculiar ways
not questioning my exit
to back yard or parking lot
where I search the sky
for their awkward gyre.

I spy them in their ragged line
that soon breaks apart
like leaves in a gust of wind,
circling around no stable center,
each of them possessed
by a leisure or confusion
they should not be able to afford
while escaping winter.

I have watched them by the thousands
feeding in picked fields,
all leg and neck,
red masks fit for the dance
they do
like TV puppets,
always amazing me how they thrive
despite Nature's disdain
for silliness
and this rampant Earth
Man has made.

CUBAN MISSILE CRISIS ANXIETY

Lunch in a brown paper bag, eating in the bleachers,
reading my *Lord of the Flies*,
the other kids loud, but not enough to hide
the sudden sirens in the distance only I can hear.
I try not to move too fast across the basketball court,
its circle a bullseye, push the bar on the exit door,
the runaway elevator I'm trapped on never reaching bottom.
Outside I sprint to the edge of the playground,
look west where steel mills never stop smoking
and the Nike base, with its white-finned rockets,
guards against those slow bombers of another era.
Just beyond the curve of the earth Chicago is the prize.
I estimate the minutes it will take
for grinning Khrushchev's missiles
to cross the Early Warning Line,
and how many more until the people,
now alert in the streets with nowhere to go,
all look up, just like me, and watch the warheads,
bright in the autumn sun, fall like Armageddon's stars.

CHILDREN OF FIRE

Once we fled
dry season fires
like other beasts,
but then
we learned
to stay along the edges,
to go back in
when the charred ground
cooled,
where there was always meat
free for taking,
so tender it pulled
from the bones,
our fingers,
still too clumsy
to fashion tools,
stroking thick brows
and furry cheeks
of our children
as we gave thanks
to the flames
with guttural refrains.

Once when lightning
struck
a baobab tree,
made it burn
from inside out,
one of us,
more clever than the rest,
stabbed a stick
into the leopard's
glowing eye
and carried fire back home,

those embers kept alive
in mud-lined gourds
for the next camp,
and the next,
where we held the night

at bay,
filled our bellies
and sang.

The sun and the moon,
the earth, the water,
and the wind
we learned to praise
as we spread,
but fire was our

Mother,
and when we were ready
she taught us
to strike
two blades of flint together,
her spark,
the shooting star,
guiding us still.

RAINWATER HAIR

All that rain and I happened to be there,
my grandmother's big house on the corner
with brown asphalt siding and the mock orange in bloom,
the coal stove in the front room cold now,
mica pane without that winter glow
from bright burning anthracite.

My grandmother in one of the printed dresses
she always wore, her gray hair long in braids,
and my aunt with her iron bun held by pins,
and her teenage daughter, her white blond
Shirley Temple curls no barrette could tame,
all three grabbing metal buckets
and rushing through the thunder
to the down spout gushing next to the porch,
telling me to bring more pots from the kitchen
as theirs got filled with foamy harvest.

"We wash our hair in rainwater,"
my cousin explained as the storm passed
as fast as it had come,
my aunt more happy than I'd ever seen her,
my grandmother dipping a juice glass and handing it to me,
"Drink it," she said, "It will make you tall and handsome."

Rain tasted of lightning and flint with a hint of coal smoke
and the deep spot in the creek back home
where my friends and I would dive.

My cousin said it was important
to use the rain right after it had fallen,
and the three of them left me with my comic books
on the living room couch,
and soon I could hear
the sound of laughing and splashing
drifting down the stairs.

I watched the sky clear through the bay window
where my grandma had placed a jar of green sun tea
that she would later sweeten with A&P honey

and sip while she listened to her giant wooden radio
with its golden dial,
her rainwater hair smelling of baby shampoo
and spreading in a silver fan
across her clean silk blouse,
her foot tapping to Dixieland jazz

CHIMNEY SWIFTS AT DUSK

At dusk
the sky is filled
with wings.

My hotel window
on the highest floor
presents a timeworn city

built of brick and stone,
chimneys that once
belched smoke

now wait for them to return,
these sleek birds, black as soot,
mad to devour

the last mosquito and moth.
The tall stack of an old factory
across the street

blurs as I watch
the swifts spin
like a whirlwind,

then become a genie
funneled back into its lamp
when a dark hand

conjures day to a starry end.

CORN TRUCK OVERTURNS ON MAIN STREET

Semi-trailer filled from silos,
tidal wave of last year's golden crop.
Traffic stopped, doorways blocked,
old men in the coffee shop

tapping their canes on glass
excited to be trapped.
Baby in its stroller, wide eyes
filled with so much yellow,

some yahoo in a four-wheel drive
plows in, does doughnuts,
spraying kernels like hail and bullets,
sheriff stays in his cruiser

remembering a convoy
and a roadside bomb.
Someone flies their drone
to document this news

where news never happens,
climbing up above
camera sweeps around
to capture endless fields

freshly tilled, waiting to be planted,
and down on the road
a pastor on his bike,
heading out of town

on a long ride
to get his sermon right,
imagining August,
his favorite month,

with tall corn
for miles and miles,
hot and sighing
with Nature's breath.

SUNNY MORNING AFTER THE BIG BLIZZARD

The weight of it
settled and still,

the world quiet
except for birds
around their feeder,

and the furnace
like the engine
of a submarine.

There is nowhere to go
until the plows come;

here, suddenly,
our prayers answered,

cozy refugees
marooned together,

snow waist high
against the kitchen door.

ODE TO SAND
(Indiana Dunes)

> Henry Chandler Cowles, at the University of Chicago, developed a more formal concept of succession. Cowles studied vegetation development on the ever moving sand dunes on the southern shores of Lake Michigan (the Indiana Dunes). He first published this work as a paper in the Botanical Gazette in 1899 ("The ecological relations of the vegetation of the sand dunes of Lake Michigan").
> —Wikipedia

1.
Imagine the journey sand makes,
ten thousand years,
jewels the ice sheet lost
melting into a new sea,
water sweet as rain,
nature's most patient mill
grinding its meal of quartz.

2.
Waves deliver it here,
grain upon grain.
Free, it cannot rest.
It erases our footprints,
steals the dropped key,
mars the lovers' damp skin,
hides inside the shoes
worn home.

3.
Marram grass was the first
to find a way to grow in sand,
it's bending in the breeze
a koan as we walk through.
The cottonwoods next
know the sand will give them nothing.
They spread their roots,
thrust toward the sun,
will not be buried.
In the heat of June
the sand is rife
with snowy seeds.

The jack pines, backing up,
ragged fighters
ever green with spite,
always hungry—
their armored cones dream of fire,
waiting to explode.

4.
They work in tandem,
wind and sand,
remembering former spells, epochs,
barren times loved best,
cataclysmic skies, rains of cinders,
the sun choked by vapor and ash,
droughts and conflagrations,
ice pushing in from the poles,
life driven back to its margins,
hiding as the inanimate world
resumes its rightful rule.

5.
We climb the front of the dune
using a path that curves around
the blowout shaped like a theater
where music is played,
a few ancient trees, whittled down,
brittle and gray,
stand exposed once more
at the back where the wind
off the water
lifts the sand uphill.

6.
On top the high dune is rippled, ribbed,
sand blowing around our ankles,
its tickle, its tease
never betraying its true intention.
Behind us Lake Michigan
fills half the world,
before us, the land lays flat,

the confident green of summer,
fecund, abounding, singing,
never questioning its place.

7.
The dune demands we learn to fly,
steep and sliding on the leeward side,
bounding like those men on the moon.
The old house at the bottom
is nearly entombed,
front porch strangled by wild grape.
We can still see where the parlor was,
the sand pouring in
when the roof collapsed,
floorboards covered,
the message
a lizard scrawled there,
and a coyote's meal,
bones waiting to be cast.

ORANGE

There were no oranges to buy
when I was an Indiana,
nineteen fifties child,
not like today
piled at the supermarket
with the apples and potatoes.

There was only the orange in the stocking
I received at church on Christmas Eve,
an orange the color of a rising sun,
warm and smooth in my hands,
its smell when peeled
an explosion of light
and happiness,
that magic little world
I separated into pieces and shared
back home
like Jesus taught,

its juice in my mouth
so tart, yet wildly sweet,
but the seeds, if you bit them,
bitter as the wages of sin.

ANCESTORS

We walked through the barnyard
rowdy with geese and chickens.
Uncle John,
my grandmother's oldest brother,
opened the wooden gate
into a pasture sloping gently
into the past,
the grazing horses he employed
around the farm
raised their heads
to look at us,
an old man in overalls and the boy
who relished how lucky he was
to have traveled back in time
on that Sunday afternoon.

I was too young
to boldly ask
why he and his brother
chose to live that way,
no power lines
marching down the dirt lane
into their house,
the washer with a crank
on the front porch,
those kerosene lamps,
without a genie,
smudged with soot
and the smell of coal oil
always in the air,
a reminder
of how much effort
it must take
with no buttons to push
or switches to flick.

John led me
across the land
my ancestors cleared,
the Michigan Road

cut through virgin forest
bringing them in by the wagon load
from Ohio and Kentucky
with their rough hands
and Bibles,
their tools forged by blacksmiths
making miracles happen,
their lye soap and prayers
stronger than any fear.
John took it from his deepest pocket,
a rod shaped like an L
with an elderberry handle,
hollow, I was told,
so the iron could spin
if so inspired.
"This ditch witch
can find underground streams
better than a willow fork,"
he explained,
and I followed him,
the skeptic seed
already sprouted
just below my politeness
and respect.

We walked in zigzags,
the device inert
in his gnarled hand.
I was thinking what to say
when we found no buried water
and I lagged behind
among the thistles,
their flowers blue and painful,
until I saw him motion
and I ran to his side.
The rod had begun to circle,
as he knew it would,
faster with each turn.
"There's a powerful flow down there,"
he said.

"Here, you take over now."
As I held it, spinning hard,
with those two small hands,
still in disbelief,
my heart beating in my chest,
what could I have understood
about blood,
pushing steady and unstoppable
through the ages.

DISHWASHER

The kitchen crazy at his back,
clatter, shouts, profanity,
bangs and trash talk
interspersed with fire.

Filthy plates and silverware,
dirty water glasses and the sommelier's picks,
all flow back with the current
and gather where he mans his post,
the big machine humming,
so hot and steamy he never gets dry.

Servers in black and white
enter and exit, plead with the line,
their clocks running out,
the expediter sliding
back and forth like a ninja,
prime time a battle in candlelight,
bussers rolling in with loaded carts
jammed into his corner.
He knows the marathon runner's steady pace
in a white sleeveless t-shirt,
tattoo snake coiled around a knife,
red bandana to keep his head on.

The staff sits out at the bar
after the doors close,
but he's still finishing pots and pans
when the chef brings him
a fat glass
of Tennessee whisky
and shakes his hand

that at least warms his walk home
to the little apartment
with its single dresser,
the top drawer, his dress blues
neatly folded and the Purple Heart.

CANADA GEESE

Feet splayed, leather between toes,
black claws meant for pedestrian tasks,
you meet me with your mate in the office parking lot.

Though there's something regal in your head held high,
I've seen you eating grass on suburban lawns,
your hungry bill opening and closing as I approach,
greeting me like you were my pet.

Once I watched you overhead, migrating spring and fall,
symbol of everything wild I loved
as a boy pushed toward an artificial world.
Now the comfort of retention ponds, of parks and city heat,
has erased your need to cross those distances,
the magnet sky of yours still lit with guiding lines and fluxes.

Even those of us who welcome you
notice how you've swelled in numbers,
how you stop the traffic
as you trundle across these busy streets
as though they belong to you.
Many others loathe what you've become,
look at you as some king size pigeon,
another pest dug in to stay and complicate our crude ballet.

How you watch me so directly with those black pearl eyes
when I reach to touch you, to rub your head
with a loving finger—you snap your beak,
your pink tongue wagging,
and remind me that your distant kin
were brontosaurus and T-rex,
warning me away with your baby dragon's hiss.

THE CREEK

A single shallow creek
flowed through
those plain flat fields,

but gave us
all we needed,

its banks
a hint of wilderness,
free from prying
adult eyes,

our wigwams
built of sticks
and sumac fronds,

cub scout knives
to sharpen willow spears,

flint and steel
to light a fire,

the deep spot
where we dove.

I will always know
the snapping turtle's
golden eyes,

the kingfisher's cackle
and splash,

the water snake
that made us scatter,

how we dreamt
we'd cross the ocean,
or travel
back in time,

to lands more welcoming
of boys
with tiger stripes
of mud.

ROAD

Once we followed the others on all fours,
contributing trails through grass and brush
to favorite trees and watering holes
before our spines thrust us up on two feet,
gave us a taste for meat and tools and weapons,
the flame growing ever brighter between our eyes.

We sang to guide us along the lines we dreamed,
familiar landmarks, then continents, taming horses, camels,
the mighty aurochs turned to beast of burden,
the buffalo wading through rice with drooping horns,
saddles and reins and heavy yokes pulling plows,

and when the wheel came spinning down from the stars
it would not be long until path became road,
villages, towns, cities, the maps of empires
drawn on hide and parchment in ink and blood,
commerce and legions, Mesopotamia and India
paving with stone, the Romans linking half the world,
Via Appia lined with cypress, herbs and ruins,
still there after 2000 years.

The bulldozers push through red sand on the way
to something precious, a mine where we will fill
another need, a highway wider than the rest,
rushing west at ever faster speed toward a setting sun.

OLD SYCAMORE

The tree enchants the riverbank,
so wide, gnarled and hollow,
its skin beneath the shedding bark
a mottled map, an abstract painter's
canvas, its limbs and branches
turning white as bone as it climbs,
crowding out the neighbors
to display that ivory crown.

I duck through the entrance
in its side, stand in a space
filled with light from constellations,
the holes of birds with chisel beaks,
look up where the heartwood
feeds rot and ants moving
toward the sky, put my hand
on brittle xylem still alive with sap
rising to a galaxy of star shaped leaves
and thorny fruits as centuries pass.

BOAT HULL MOVING PARTY IN A SMALL TOWN

It lifts off supports that have held it
since the dream lit on paper,
charming time from father and son,
now years and their secret kept hidden
from the town until the invitation,
word of mouth and flyers stuck
in all the right places.
It is heavy but not the way we thought,
keel slicing dim air inside the barn as it moves,
door sliding open to the bright afternoon
and the volleyball net, the silver kegs,
the loaded picnic tables and barbeque grills,
a party until now. We are ancient again,
linked by this burden, our strength together
enough to flip the boat onto the trailer,
no deck or cabin yet, no masts, no wheel
or rudder to steer into the purest stretch of sea;
we have only that horizon we imagine,
our mistakes and regrets dwindling fast behind us,
every future ideal as we all step back and applaud.

RUNNING THE TRAILS AT EAGLE CREEK

(Eagle Creek in Indianapolis is one of the largest municipal parks in the U.S.)

After the snow has melted
and the mud dried
the trails are passable again
and I can still see the blue sky
bright through bare branches as I run,
escaping a city that wants me gone.

I am a hunter's son
who still needs to know
the name of every plant and animal,
the meaning of each sight, sound and scent
spelled out in code
by Nature's wild encyclopedia.

This kind of winter morning
is made for birds,
loud and busy, thriving in cold
with their naked feet and legs,
the little ones scolding me
as they strip away bark and scatter leaves.

A pileated woodpecker
lands on a sycamore trunk,
his crazy eye in its stripe
underneath a clown's red thatch
looking down to inspect me
before he begins to hammer,
the forest echoing with his drum.

Ahead of me crows gather
around an owl asleep in a pine,
their normal circumspection
lost to sudden rage,
revenge a black storm
through the trees where predator and prey
have traded places in their acrobatic weave.

As I near the lake I can hear
the calls of sand hill cranes,
and when I come out on the shore
the sky is filled with their rippling waves,
geese and gulls gathered to witness
on patches of ice, a foretelling,
a promise, perhaps, the center will always hold.

My watch tells me I must head back,
the jagged shards of urban life

smoothed a little half way out,
and in the lot as I unlock my car
an eagle banks across the sun,
returned from limbo to soar again
over subdivisions and interstates.

I watch it circle, then come down low
to bless me.

THE OLD MAN SPEAKS AT COMMENCEMENT

You cannot stay here.
There is no longer room.
If I had my powers back
I'd throw dirt
at the sun and make
a world for you,
bright settlers
hanging from parachutes,
little books of poetry
about where you come from
hidden in your pockets
instead of tools,
caution and inspiration
and pride
tossing seeds around
waiting to see what grows.

SWARM

(green darners feeding)

Every evening
they draw me down to the water
where I stretch out my arms
with my head bent back
and stand in the center of a storm,
thousands of dragonflies,
flitting, darting, circling,
coming so close I can
hear their wings,
a hum, a hungry wind
against my skin,
this spectacle I long to join,
another bejeweled dancer
moving to a symphony
written on the air,
our appetite never satisfied,
the score of life performed
by every cell.

FOUR HAIKU

leaning down to drink
young crow tries in vain to steal
his own shiny eye

cherry tree in bloom
I take refuge under you
falling petals tears

rose potatoes cut
revealing butter gold flesh
water heats in pot

this year spring comes late
green spears thrusting through dead leaves
buds will soon explode

CROWS

> "They're out to protect their family and their neighborhood and they don't do anything alone or quietly. They're more like people than any other animal on earth"
> —Dr. Kevin McGowan

I am watched, running trails
through disturbed territory.
They do not know my name
but my shape and intent
have been transferred
through the treetops
by their harsh vocabulary,
passing me on
from station to station,
wary and wise
from hawks and owls
and armed men who think
in terms of thieves.

Back at the lot,
mine is the only car,
but I see them already gather
on the low branches
wishing me gone.

I open the trunk
and from the grocery sack
pay toll for my passage
with bread and berries.

LEG CRAMP AT NIGHT

awakened
gunshot seed
surprised in flesh,

sudden jagged bloom,

trigger flower,
my limp all day

BLOODROOT

The bloodroot is blooming. Ivory clumps of guiltless blossoms shine among tumbled blocks of limestone.

Halting my journey, I can't keep my eyes from the old quarry walls that shelter this wildflower garden. How easy to imagine a lost city fallen into ruin, grand foundations dripping cold water, towers reduced to rubble where ferns and trees now thrive. The Romans believed every place to have a genius loci, a guardian spirit. A breeze whispers in my ear.

Thoreau wrote: "A town is saved, not more by the righteous men in it than by the woods and swamps that surround it." Back then America was still an uncrowded land, its greatest cities tiny by today's standards. An urban dweller in 1844 could find Thoreau's brand of salvation at the end of a walk or buggy ride.

We are a race too easily enchanted by the ring of the ax. Our first written story is the epic of Gilgamesh, who cut down the trees where the Gods lived.

I take the path that leads to the top of a cliff and look out over my city's botanical gardens. Through budding leaves the conservatory gleams like an emperor's palace.

This is a young city in a young land. We move through lives so fast, changing scenery like stage sets. These acres below have had been many things in a short time—Indian land and hardscrabble farm, cemetery and sanitarium, rock mine and golf course.

As I walk back down into the spent quarry, past bloodroot and hepatica, past shooting star and Jacob's ladder and Solomon's seal, I think of that which cannot be hauled away in wagons and railroad cars, that which the bulldozers cannot uncover, no matter how much they rearrange.

Righteous men do save the world. They become gardeners.

Steve Brammell grew up in rural Indiana which gave him a keen appreciation of the natural world and agriculture. As a young boy his father taught him the name of every plant and animal he came into contact with in the woods and fields around his home. He attended high school in Michigan City, on the shores of Lake Michigan, and graduated from Wabash College, where he took part in the Counter Culture revolution of the late 1960s and early 70s. While there he also developed an appreciation for the traditional liberal arts as well as the study of other cultures and the sciences.

He has traveled widely, acquiring a fascination with food and wine which turned into a career later in life. He was first employed in the mental health field, then as a freelance writer specializing in technical and medical writing. He began writing for magazines in the 1990s. He has worked in the culinary world for the last twenty-five years, the past ten in the wine business.

His poems and short stories have appeared in a number of literary journals. He was nominated for a Best of the Net Award in 2021 by the Indiana Writers Center. His short story collection, *Red Mountain Cut*, was published by Finishing Line Press. He is currently writing a long historical novel set in the dune country on the southern shore of Lake Michigan.

www.ingramcontent.com/pod-product-compliance
Lightning Source LLC
Chambersburg PA
CBHW022125090426
42743CB00008B/1003